Nothing But Lace

Poetry by kc

KC Gloer's Collection of Passion

Poetry

2-1-2019

Mark,
You are a very nice person. It is my pleasure to know you!
KC

Acknowledgements

I want to thank Sharon Henifin, Co-Founder, Breast Friends, a non-profit helping women who have been diagnosed with breast, ovarian and all women's cancers. Sharon, who is a woman who has dedicated her life to helping other women, is the reason I was able to get my life back. Through her caring and sensitivity she knew I was broken, a woman living in silence for thirty years from a horrific abusive life. She helped me to regain my self-esteem, my life, my energy to break free.

Sharon helped me to format and publish this book with her technical skills presenting this elegant book for you to enjoy.

Our lives were connected forever the day I walked in, May 2013 and proceeded to work with this organization for 1½ years. Sharon, changed my life, Breast Friends, changed my life. In giving back, I found myself. In listening to women's stories, I started to share mine.

Special Quote

"When a poetess writes sensual verses she would unfold a greater thing that echoes far beyond the physical where her yet-to-be-satiated spiritual thirst navigate the existence in search for the real value of love, the all-embracing sense of warmth and the very essence of beauty immortal. Such everlasting experiences secure their origin and its essence deep in the innermost of her melodically throbbing heart. Kasey's poetry is a perfumed path, waving up and down in response to the rhythm of that heartbeat to head out for a horizon where the dawning sun of a future success smiles wide"

George Onsy
Prof. at the Egyptian-Russian University in Cairo (ERU) History of Art & Architecture Writer, poet and artist Icon of Peace from WIP, Nigeria 2017 Laureate by the WIP with the award:

'THE WORLD MOST OUTSTANDING PEACE POET FOR 2017'

Dedication

This will come as a surprise to her but I want to dedicate this book to my sister Sandra Beth Peabody who will be with me for eternity. She has always supported my writing, been there for me and my son when she didn't know what was going on in my life but has the most generous loving heart and I know has always wanted the best for my son and I. I love you Sand, forever and always.

Also, my mother, Janice who deserves a book written about her, which I also plan on doing. This woman has loved me, without judgement, my entire life…I owe her so much…if you get a special place in heaven for helping other people … that is where she will be, she has lived her life in service of others. She probably won't have time to read this as she will be swimming, dancing, biking, and camping or with her church groups. Still at 88 years old she calls me and tells me to get up and go for a walk like she does every morning! I love you more than any words can say

mom

Opening Remarks

I wish for this book to take you places that you long to be, maybe have forgotten about, or just escaping to for a moment. That is why I wrote these poems.

Please come with me on this journey of passion and life through chapters of "Dreaming, Getting Ready, Seduction and Lace Undone" I promise you there will be more to come.

Chapters

Dreaming of Romance

Poems

Dreamy Places Be

In the Deep of the Night

Escaping into the Night

I See You

Breathing Life

I Dare Not Move

To Dream

Warm Pillow

Dreaming

With the Night Comes Peace

Journey Slow

As you Sleep, I Lay Awake

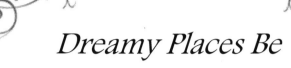

Dreamy Places Be

Although
We are worlds away
You are near to me
When I say
I feel your warmth
Your tender touch
Your love
That you give to me so much

Tonight
As you hold me close to you
Feel my heartbeat
As I do you
Sleep in dreamy places be
As I hold your hand
As you lay next to me
With your lips resting
Upon my cheek
No words
Do we have to speak
When eyes softly close
Mystery abounds

In sleepy, dreamy places be

Holding your hand

Next to me

Tasting your lips

Sweet and divine

Oh baby, come to me

In this dream of mine

In the Deep of the Night

I wait for this time
In the deep of the night
Illusions surround me
My mind starts to write

Only now can I breathe
Can I dream, can I feel
For the verse to evolve
As my heart starts to heal
The darkness of night
Transcends slow then too fast
As I drift off to sleep
To let go of the past.

Reflections

Escaping Into the Night

I wait each day
for the nighttime to take me to you
To see your face
feeling your hands caressing my back
To feel your lips,
upon my neck
To have you gently sway me
back and forth
Getting closer and closer
gentle yet so strong you feel

Calmness taking over

Then you hold my face
as you kiss me ever so softly
I feel your lips
move down and down
As you move even lower
I am filled with desire like never before
Escaping into the night
is where I want to be
Feeling you close to me
deeply close
If only in a dream

I See You

So dark Is the night
You still speak to me
When I drift off to sleep
I know you are there,
why?
Because I can see you
Sense you
As I close my eyes
You will appear

Breathing Life

Breathing life
Welcoming the night
Moon so full
Such a sensuous glow
Powerfully wanting you
Come to me
Hear my plea
Please, come to me
Feverishly
Love me
When you come to me
I will breathe life into you
To last

For all eternity

Reflections

I Dare Not Move

Stillness of the night
Very, very dark
Yet a sliver of light
Magnifies your beauty
I dare not move
Keeping you in view
Until you fade away
At the dawn of the day.

To Dream

To dream is to live
So live out your dreams
Whispering in darkness
Is the night what it seems
Dreams in the night
Bring to life what you wished
Dreams in the light
Are dreams not to be missed
I fall asleep with excitement
Waiting for dreams to unfold
What will be my enticement
When the night turns so cold
As I awake with the sunshine
Warming my face
I know the world is mine
It is ready for my embrace
My dreams made it clear
It is up to me don't you see
To live my dreams from the night
To be free

To be all that I can be

Warm Pillow

A soft voice
Gentle words
As I close my eyes
Do I hear
Come to me
As I lie
Upon my pillow
Warmth I feel
Tenderly
Your touch
Tranquility
Sensitivity
Ecstasy
Oh, dreams at play
Warmly
On this pillow
Where I lie
Where I may
Think
Dream
Of the possibility
You holding me tight

Whispering
Warmly
Come to me

Lie here
On my pillow
If just for this once
If just for now
Come to me

Dreaming

Dreaming of dancing
All night long
Dreaming of romancing
Until the coming of dawn
Dreaming of the sunlight
So beautiful on your face
Dreaming of your kiss
Morning of tenderness
Dreaming of your touch
When you don't want to leave
Dreaming of the warmth
Of your breath on my skin
Dreaming of this feeling
To be alive once again

With the Night Comes Peace

With the night comes peace
Silence so sweet
Fingertips dreaming
While my eyes defy sleep.

Journey Slow

Awake we dream
Of glorious nights
To close our eyes
When we're kissed goodnight

To capture the warmth
We all should feel
Sending you places
Passion so real

If tonight you're alone
Then dream instead
Of the one you wish
To be sharing your bed

Journey to places
You dare not go
Journey beyond
And journey slow

Journey to where
Your dreams are told
Take this journey
When the nights turn cold.

As You Sleep, I Lay Awake

As you sleep, I lay awake
As you dream, I write
Of fantasies fulfilled
About passions of the night

Reflections

Getting Ready for You

Poems

Make it Hot

Getting Ready for You

Satin

Begin Again

Passionate Sea

Eyes of the Moon

Wicked Thoughts

Run to Me

Make it Hot

I'm in the mood to take a bath
With lots of bubbles and tea on hand
Make it hot and steamy too
Where I will pamper myself
Getting ready for you

Reflections

Getting Ready for You

Royally deep, majestic hues
Welcoming, as the evening ensues
Breathing in sweetness, a tickling mist
Anticipating, wanting, your seductive kiss

With playful eyes, choosing a dress
Just low enough to show off my best
Blue royal blue, shimmering hot
Elegance flows, boring I'm not

Freshly powdered, sensual perfume
Silky golden curls, I assume
As they softly fall, warming my neck
Invite your lips to seductively peck

A single pearl, so perfectly placed
What's underneath, **_Nothing But Lace_**
Thighs revealed, yet never too much
Letting you know, I long for your touch

Clear glass slippers, alas I am through
The rest of the evening, is all up to you
Let's sway with the music, sexily slow
Until our desires, crescendo and grow
Ok, I am ready, it's time, let's go!

Satin

The feel of satin
On my skin
Breathing the fragrance
So divine it's a sin
Tonight is the night
Let the loving begin.

Begin Again

It's over.
Quiet
I lay still
Exhilarated
Breathing rapid
A drop reaches my spine
Gliding gently
Down and down
The curves of my spine
My body glistening
Every part
Listening to my heart beat
My eyes are closed
Clear my mind
Absorb this moment
Captivated by the power
The strength
The intensity
Now I am ready
Ready to begin

Passionate Sea

Passionate fingers
Passionate lips
Passionate waves
Upon the cliffs

Hear my song
Through the waves of time
Hear my song
As the seagulls climb

An ocean apart
Is not far at all
When your souls dive deep
When they hear the call

Feeling the emotion
Like a raging tide!
Swallowing the potion
Mysteries confide
Let go,
Just be swept away
Let go,
Just be eternally free
Let go.
Just make love in the passionate sea.

Eyes of the Moon

Oh, the glow fading soon
Calm is upon us
As will be
The eyes of the moon
Tranquility in the sky
Mystery of the trees
Whispering
Walk on by
Come to me
Breathe in my leaves
Feel my strength
Of my limbs on thee
The breeze will caress
Swirling your hair
The mist hovering
A little more a little less
Listening
To the sounds of the night
Hearing, come to me, come
This is our time
Under the moonlight
Magnificent
Breathtakingly alive

Wicked Thoughts

My thoughts are wicked tonight
The dark is darker then dark
As the wild cry out for their mates
No hint of the moonlight in sight

I put on my sheer flowing top
That barely reaches my thighs
With my hair falling just to my breasts
This night is not going to stop

As your eyes gaze upon my hips
I feel such ecstasy
Your hand slides somewhere deep
While your mouth caresses my lips

I love the way that you taste
I love the passion in your finger tips
You are sending me to a wondrous place
Come with me, there's no time to waste

Run to Me

When you're lonely
Think of me
I will talk to you
Keep you company

When you're sad
Reach for me
I will hold your hand
Compassionately

When you're tired
Come to me
I will kiss your eyes
Sing you a lullaby

When you need comfort
Rest with me
I will keep you warm
lovingly heavenly

When you need love
Lay with me
I will touch your body
Gently tenderly

When you need passion

Run to me

I will reach your soul

Seductively completely

Reflection

_____

_____

_____

_____

_____

_____

_____

_____

_____

_____

Seduction

Poems

Take Me

At First Sight

Oh, A Kiss is a Kiss

Paradise All Our Own

Tasting Seduction

The Moon Appears

Wildly Sweet

Your Night

The Finest Wine

The Seduction

Touch Me

Take Me

Sing to me your song of love
Of roses, kisses and wine
Sing to me your song so tender
Of midnight swims intertwined
Sing to me your song of love
Of midnight touches so divine

Hold me close, so close this night
Walk me through the depths of time
Taste my lips and dance with me
Take me to where I've never been
Hold me close, so close this night
Take me now and take me sweet

Listening to your soothing voice
You guide me, sway me,
While you sing to me
Midnight blues transfixed on you
Passion swirls under the crescent moon
We will be set free, as you sing to me

At First Sight

Entering the galleria
In an instant you knew
You knew a dream you dreamed
Was going to come true
The lady of the night
Wearing elegant **black lace**
Hair of gold
Flowing down her back
A delicate chain
Dropping
In the crevice of her chest
Her cheek bones high
Shimmering rosy color
Eyes bluish green
Wide open to her soul
As she looked up
Feeling your attraction
Taking in a deep breath
Knowing what would happen
So comfortable it seemed
Yet hearts were beating fast
As you held her hand in yours
You lightly kissed her lips
Only then did you ask her name
Then you whispered in her ear
You're the one I want
The very one I've searched for

Take a chance on love
If only for one night
This night may turn into forever
Or the best memory of your life
It's in the moment we live
We live to love
We love to live
So live and love tonight!

Oh, a Kiss is a Kiss

You can make love or have sex
But a kiss, oh a kiss is a kiss
Sex can be just having sex
But that kiss, oh that kiss
Well now that is true bliss

To embrace one another this way
Is as intimate as it can be
There are no words that you can say
That brings you this close to me

When you look into my eyes
Standing over me
Brushing my hair from my face
I feel my heart start to race

Then you tilt your head a bit
As I look up at you
That is when our lips meet
That is when your heart starts to beat

My mouth on yours
As you explore even more
Lightly touching my cheek
I am trembling, I am weak

Your lips are soft and tender
Your arms are strong yet gentle
Your emotion takes over you
As you warm me through and through

Now you know why
A kiss is more than a kiss
Why it is more intimate
Why you don't want to miss

Oh, a kiss is a kiss is a kiss

Paradise All Our Own

Walk through that door
Where no one has to know
What the two of us will share
Together, all alone

This paradise all our own

Instantly at ease
Barefoot, exploring about
You prepare a cup of tea
With aromas of such delight

Selected you did, just for this night

While you stretch out on the couch
I look at you, looking at me
Knowing the pleasures that lie ahead
A little music to set the mood

I play for you, soft and smooth

Quiet, not wanting to speak
Just being present,
Hearing our hearts beat
Sipping, savoring, breathing in
Tasting, wanting, is how we begin

Tasting Seduction

Sometimes sweet
Sometimes so mellow, succulent
As it flows between my lips, around my tongue
I have waited for this moment
To hold and smell your rich fragrance
To see the shimmering of the deepest red
Through the magnificence of your crystal
Oh the warmth of its potion
And the seduction of its power
Now I am ready to fall under your spell
Take me to that place
Where an evening to remember awaits

Reflection

The Moon Appears

A cloudless night
Brilliance nothing less

Secrets to confess

Enchanted breeze
Calling to me

Sensing your presence

Flowing so free
Connected by the moon

Heightened intensity

Dissolving all time
Heartbeats on mine

Your silhouette excites

Through the moonlight
Pure Magnificence

Pure delight
Into your grasp

Wildly Sweet

You opened a door
At this moment in time
Needing your touch
As you extended your hand
All was quiet, caring and calm
Daringly seductive, music played on
Trusting you, needing you
Now letting go
To passions revived
From so long ago
On and on, the fires did churn
Intensity soared, just craving more
A day with no ending
A night just beginning
The perfect seduction
Wildly sweet

Your Night

I will come to you
As you lie sleeping
Dreaming, knowing
Your dream is not a dream

Deep in the dusk
Sensations are dancing
Keeping eyes closed
Reality or imagined?

The moonlight shines bright
You know it is true
This is not a dream
I have come to you

To pleasure and treasure
All that you are
This night, all night
Belongs just to you

Reflections

The Finest Wine

Let your fingers be hungry
While your mouth explores gently
Your lips slightly parted
Gliding your tongue against mine

Savoring the flavors
Like a fine sip of wine
Slowly and carefully
Taking your time

Your hands intertwined
In the strands of my hair
Caressing my face
Gently with care

Your hips against mine
As you pull me even closer
Still, so tenderly kissing
Treating me as fragile as glass

Seducing my mind,
My body, my all
Surrendering completely
When you love so sweetly

Taking you deeply
Heaven releasing
Showing you too
The joy of this feeling

The Seduction

You held my hand
Then took a sip
Upon your lips
I tasted and licked

Romantic music
Jazzy blues set the beat
Pulling me close
You rose with the heat

Dancing, romancing
Loving your moves
Strumming, humming
This mood does soothe

Your instrument? Just me,
Playing your song
Soulfully, on my body
All wonderfully night long

Reflections

Touch Me

Touch my cheek, my legs go weak,
Kiss my lips with such tenderness,
Hold me close,
Let your desires go,
Devour my soul,
You will never let go

Lace Undone

Poems

Aroused by the Moonlight

Tenderness to Passion

Allured by the Storm

Intensity Rising

Crave

Feeling it Coming

Discovering Secrets

Heartbeat

Passions of the Dark

Read my Heart

Breathe You While I Sleep

Aroused by the Moonlight

It's quiet, yet not
Your footsteps draw near
Moonlight arouses the night
I see you so clear

My body is shivering
Yet my passions on fire
Your eyes seduce me
I feel your desire

I have dreamt of your touch
Your warmth and your lips
Caressing my face
Your hips on my hips

Feel me, all of me
As you dive deep inside
Pleasures await you
I'll kiss the tears you have cried

I'll hear your emotion
Your soul will be free
When you give of yourself
On this night spent with me.

Tenderness to Passion

To lie with you
To touch you
Rhythms of the night
A chill of anticipation
Silk caressing my body
Heaving up and down
With each intense breath
Incredible tenderness
Your hand barely touching me
As it glides across my skin
Sweetness of your kisses
Upon my wanting shoulder
Warmth rising from within
Getting ready for the storm
Music so alive
Exciting me, seducing me
As your tongue is wet and wild
Tenderness to passion
Just like I imagined
Crossing the boundary
Without even knowing
How it all began

Allured by the Storm

Crashing and swirling
Storms allure me
Take me with your swell
Show me
Teach me
What you do so well
Take me now!

Intensity Rising

Fiery skies mirrored in calmness
A feeling of peace
As passions increase
Intensity rising
Hypnotizing
Falling into tranquil sleep

Crave

Moody, foggy, mysterious night
Snow looms high
No rain in sight

Slowly, softly whispering low
Your deepest desires
How far will you go?

Sexily, smoothly kissing begins
Tasting your flavors
Giving all to win

Sweetness, tenderness, passion grows
Hungrily amazing
Of love it flows

Shaking, moaning desires rage
Flesh on flesh
Craving what you crave

Deepening, soulfully out of control
Euphoria in unison
Contentment now full

Feeling it Coming

Seduced by the seas
Emerald green and white
Thrilling such passions
Sounds of delight

With powerful thrusts
Lightening does strike
Anticipating the thunder
No two are alike

Feeling it coming
At that moment of peace
Stopping all breathing
Until the silence does cease

Wild screams of pleasure
Riding waves so high
Drenched in emotion
Ravenous clouds part the sky

As the tide recedes
Stillness has won
Mysteries uncovered
With the rising sun

Birds circling in motion
Stormy seas long gone
Calmness taking over
Serenity of the dawn

Discovering Secrets

Magical eve as serenity soothes
Singing songs of love as the night ensues
Bring me your passion in a tender touch
When the moon is high, illuminating the sky

Now you can reach the erotic zones
Before only dreamt about, when all alone
Explore the depth of the softest flesh
Tasting the sweetness, on more than just breath

Immersed in ecstasy, wildly anxious
Completely vulnerable, willing to trust
Trying to wait, can't stop the explosion
The love we make, so filled with emotion

The heat is high, the wetness flows
Your spine dripping wet
Yet, your thirst not quenched
Now is when you're ready to go

Deeper into ecstasies lair
Where the screams of delight
Tell the story of passion's might
Discovering secrets never known,
until tonight

Heartbeat

In your fingertips, it beats
As you touch me
The rhythm begins
In the breeze of your breath
A chill overcomes me
You are so alive
Consumed by your excitement
Anticipating
Your drums are beating
Stronger and stronger
My heart synchronized with yours
Mesmerized by this pounding
Rising and falling
Into your heat
Smelling your energy
Musky and sweet
An ocean of passion
Together we meet
Still slowly we move
No more do we speak
Gliding and sighing
With ecstasy's own beat
Drowned in wetness
As a wave in the sea
Effortlessly beautifully
Riding so free

Can't tell
As they beat as one
Wildly fiercely
The crescendo's begun.

Passions of the Dark

Your hand rests
Between the cavern
Of my breasts
Eyes closed
Waiting
Anticipating
Where will you
Touch me next
Your lips replace your hand
While your hand
Finds another place
Of warmth and comfort
Slow
Deliberate
Carefully you touch
Wild
Passionately
Lips
I crave so much
Upon my breast
Upon my neck
Sucking, gliding
Everywhere and now
Your tongue
Is there
Circling all around
Yet still
Your hand

Is steady
Teasing
Exploring
Moaning
Wanting
Enjoying
Adoring
Magnificent you are
In the passions
Of the dark

Read My Heart

Amidst my tears
You read my heart
Silenced my cries
My lips you would part

Tightening your grip
Feelings embraced
Kissing salt from my lips
Sensually, probing my lace

The wetness of your tongue
Craving to explore
Rising up to say
I have opened the door

Come to me right now
Come with all you've got
Wanting you this much
A good girl, I am not

I will grant your every wish
I am your fantasy
You started with my heart
Tonight you will set me free

A night that has never been
So full of passion and pleasure
A level of ecstasy
Never before imagined

Instantly you knew
What I was longing for
No hesitation or pause
I shivered, then I soared

That's how it began
It was only just the start
Once you seduced
That spot in my heart

Breathe You While I Sleep

To awaken to the sunlight
The warmth of your face
Your hands across my body
Engulfed in your embrace

You surround my every being
Penetrating the heat of the sun
Into my soul you are leaving
Your spirit becoming one

Never seeing or believing
Feelings would grow this deep
Never even conceiving
I would breathe you while I sleep

The union of our bodies
Will surge a burning desire
Of heightened sensitivities
With ecstasy to feed the fire

Relaxing inside your arms
After kissing our last kiss
Feeling safe from harm
Feelings I have missed

Eyes closed now in wetness
Heartbeats are now slowing
Deep incredible tenderness
Tomorrow love keeps flowing

Reflections

Reflections

About KC Gloer

I used to write as a young girl but forgot about my passion for writing. Life takes us in many directions but ultimately our passions surface. You need to walk through that door and seize this moment when it happens!

At 17, I graduated high school looking to find a beautiful life moving from Illinois to California. I met a man at 18 who was from Georgia, got married and eighteen years later had a child, Garet, the purpose for my life. Now I think God has a purpose for both of us.

My life consisted of a wonderful job with IBM, working in Atlanta, GA, Burlington, VT, Reno, NV, Phoenix, AZ, Coppel, TX. I was in the top 2% of sales reps for the company, earning numerous recognitions for outstanding sales including National Marketing Rep of the Year. Later, I entered a variety of fields including selling advertising and life insurance so my flexibility would allow me to be at all my son's sporting events etc.

I became very ill and housebound which led me to changing my life's direction and went to work for a nonprofit organization, Breast Friends, which helps women on an emotional level deal with breast and ovarian cancer. Since 2013 I have taken my health back and now living my passion, writing and sharing my thoughts on a topic that often remains hidden or not openly discussed, passion and love.

I am an expert in this area knowing what it is like to live without Passion and Love. My hope is through my writing and coaching I will help people rediscover this special part of life.

Published and available in CD and download format:
Nothing But Lace
Passion poetry

It's All About Love
Inspirational poetry, CD only

Future Books:
Walking Into the Light
Spiritual poetry
Autobiography
Their Power is in Your Silence

"Their Power is in Your Silence" will be my future book to help people
break free of domestic violence.
You must tell someone, that is the first step.